ParentsCAN
3299 Claremont Way, Ste.3
Napa, CA 94558

Acknowledgements

Many children, parents, and teachers have helped with this book. I would like to give special thanks to the children in the book: Sarah Badillo, Emiliano Bourgois, Sophie Corley, Cory Cunningham, Stephen Cunningham, Cynthia Delgado, Jewel Halliday, Richard Hempel, Carlos Leon, Gina McNally, David Robards, Jazmin Ruiz, Lionel Toler, Amanda Vernuccio, and Jennine Wallace. Many thanks also to The Association for the Help of Retarded Children, Bank Street Family Center, The Children's Aid Society, The Lighthouse Child Development Center, The Lighthouse, Inc., New York City Public School 199, The New York League for Early Learning, The Rusk Institute of Rehabilitation Medicine Preschool and Infant Developmental Programs, and Ira Blank, Kirstin DeBear, Carmel and Carmel Ann Favale, Heidi Fox, Susan Scheer, Sybil Peyton, and Jodi Schiffman.

The name Star Bright Books and logo are trademarks of Star Bright Books.

Designed by Allen Richardson

Published by Star Bright Books
New York

Hardback ISBN: 1-887734-34-1 (previously ISBN: 1-56288-301-1)
Paperback ISBN: 1-59572-033-2
Library of Congress Catalog Card Number: 97-69607 Printed in China. 0 9 8 7 6 5 4 3 2 1

We Can Do It!

By Laura Dwight

STAR BRIGHT BOOKS

NEW YORK

My name is Gina.
I am five years old.
I have spina bifida, and
I can do lots of things.

I like to play
with my dollhouse.

I can ride my bike.

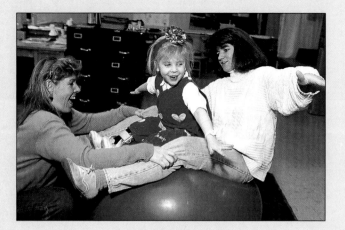

The kids want to know ▶
about my wheelchair.

▲ At school I have fun with my teachers
and my friends. ▼

▲ I push my wheelchair
to the beach because
I like to play in the sand.▶

I love the water!▶

My name is David.
I am five years old.
I have Down syndrome, and
I can do lots of things.

▼ When my friend Richard comes
over, we play with my computer.

▲Sometimes I play alone.

 ◀ I dress myself
and tie my own shoes.

▼ I help by setting the table.

I read to my little brother
and show him things.

My mom and I play games.
I'm the winner!

◀ My name is Jewel.
I am four years old.
I have cerebral palsy, and
I can do lots of things.

▲ In the greenhouse
I water the plants.

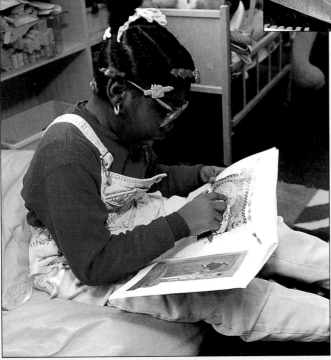

◀ I wear my new glasses
to look at books.

◀ Last year I had an operation
to help me walk.

My physical therapist ▶
helped me learn
to use a walker.

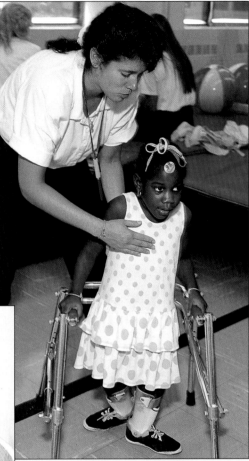

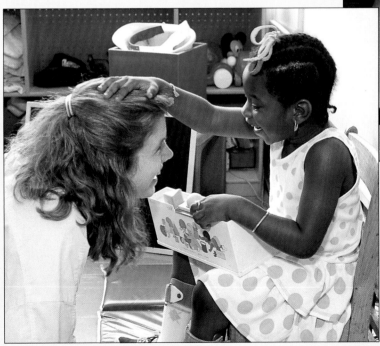

◀ I have lots of fun with
my speech therapist.

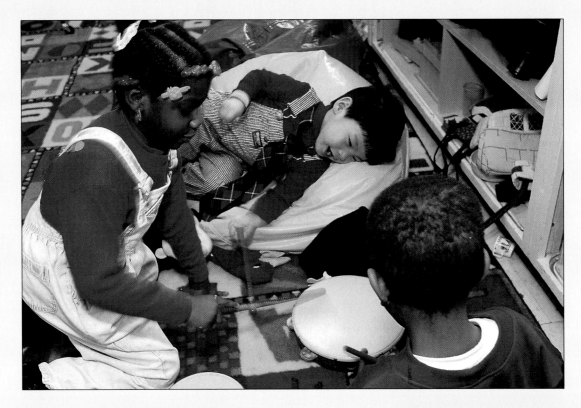

▲ At school I make music
and build things
with my friends. ▶

Cynthia and I make our puppets wrestle and shout! ▶

My name is Emiliano,
but my friends call me Nano.
I am three years old.
I have cerebral palsy,
and I can do lots of things.

When it is hot, I like to race
in and out of the sprinkler.

▲ I play with my cat.

◀ I like to have pillow
fights with my mom
and dad.

When I visit Susan, my therapist, we play games that help me stand alone and make me strong.

I am the champ! ▶

My name is Sarah.
I am four years old.
I am blind, and
I can do lots of things.

▲This is my friend Jazmin.

▲At school we play instruments and sing.

This is my chair. My name is on it in Braille. The bells help me find it. I also have bells on my right hand.

▲ I run my fingers along the wall so I can tell where I am. This is called trailing.

▲ I pour my own juice...

and clean up if it spills.

◄When my mom reads to my sister and me, I like to feel where we are in the story.

I help my dad cook—I like to make dessert! ▶

Look at all the things we can do!

◀ Cory and Amanda

▲ Carlos and Stephen

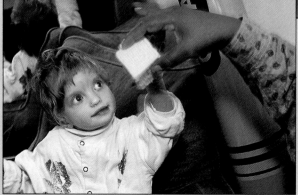

◀ Sophie

▲ Jazmin

◀Jennine ▲

Glossary

Down syndrome:
    Chromosomes are the very tiny thread-like bits in your body that tell your body how to grow. People with Down syndrome are born with one chromosome too many. A person with Down syndrome usually can do almost anything other people can do, it just might take them a little longer.

Blindness:
    A person who is blind cannot see. Some people, who can can see a little but not as well as most people, are called blind or vision-impaired. Blind and vision-impaired people use their other senses such as hearing and touch to do many things. Sometimes blind people use canes or specially-trained dogs to get around.

Spina bifida:
    Sometimes when a baby is growing inside its mother, a place along its back doesn't join up properly. When this happens, the baby's spine gets damaged and we say the baby has spina bifida. A person with spina bifida has difficulty walking but can use braces, crutches, and a wheelchair to get around.

Cerebral palsy:
    Cerebral palsy is an injury to the brain that can happen when a baby is being born. If this happens, the baby may have trouble using his or her arms or legs. People with cerebral palsy may use braces or walkers to help them walk. Some might need to use a wheelchair or a scooter to get around, and some people with cerebral palsy may need some help communicating.

RESOURCES

UNITED STATES

American Foundation for the Blind
11 Pennsylvania Plaza, Suite 300
New York, NY 10001
800-AFB-BLIN   (212) 502-7600

National Down Syndrome Congress
1605 Chantilly Drive, Suite 250
Atlanta, GA 30030
(800) 232-6372   (404) 633-1555

National Information Center for Children and
Youth with Disabilities
P.O. Box 1492, Washington D.C. 20013-1492
(202) 884-8200   (800) 695-0285

Resources for Children with Special Needs, Inc.
200 Park Avenue South, Suite 816
New York, NY 10003
(212) 677-4650
(serves New York City only)

Spina Bifida Association of America
4590 MacArthur Blvd., Suite 250
Washington, DC 20007-4226
(800) 621-3141
Information line (202) 944-3285
Fax (202) 944-3295
e-mail: spinabifida @ aol.com
web site: www.infohiway.com/spina bifida

United Cerebral Palsy Association
1660 L Street NW, Suite 700
Washington, DC 20036
(800) 872-5827
web site: http://www.ucpa.org

GREAT BRITAIN

A.S.B.A.H.
42 Park Road
Peterborough, PE1 2UQ

Downs Syndrome Association
153-155 Mitcham Road,
London SW17 9PG

REACH
Wellington House
Wellington Road
Wokingham, Berkshire RG40 2AG
Telephone: 01189891101 Fax: 01189790989
(Information for all over the world as well as U.K)

Royal National Institute for the Blind
224 Great Portland Street
London W1N 6AA

Scope
12 Park Crescent
London W1N 4EQ

AUSTRALIA

Link-Up, Education Services Section
Cultural and Educational Services
National Library of Australia, Canberra

Royal Victorian Institute for the Blind School
Burwood Highway, Melbourne, Victoria.

STAR Victoria Incorporated
Ross House, 247 Flinders Lane, 2nd Floor
Melbourne Victoria 3000
Phone: 03 9650 2730   Fax: 03 9650 6972